TREMORS OF THE EARTH:
Understanding and Surviving Earthquakes.

Esther D. Ross

ACKNOWLEDGMENT:

The completion of a book on earthquakes and resilience would not have been feasible without the invaluable assistance, mentorship, and contributions provided by numerous individuals and organizations. We express our sincere appreciation to all individuals who have contributed to the successful completion of this project.

We express our gratitude to the scientists, researchers, and experts in the fields of seismology, geology, and disaster management whose contributions serve as the basis for this book. Their unwavering commitment to comprehending earthquakes and minimizing their consequences has played a crucial role in enhancing our understanding and ability to withstand seismic hazards.

We express our gratitude to the publishers, editors, and reviewers for their invaluable feedback and support throughout the entirety of the writing and editing process. Your proficiency and meticulousness have played a crucial role in refining this book to its ultimate state.

Our gratitude is extended to the organizations and institutions that have graciously contributed data, resources, and assistance for the execution of this project. We greatly appreciate your collaboration and partnership, as they have greatly improved the quality and breadth of our research.

The resilience, courage, and perseverance demonstrated by individuals and communities impacted by earthquakes serve as a source of inspiration for us to persist in our efforts to advance earthquake awareness and preparedness. Your personal experiences and narratives serve as a poignant reminder of the significance of constructing robust communities and safeguarding lives and means of subsistence.

Finally, we express our gratitude to our families, friends, and loved ones for their steadfast support and encouragement throughout this endeavor. We greatly appreciate your patience, understanding, and encouragement, which have helped us navigate the difficulties and successes of writing this book.

Thank you to all those who have made significant and minor contributions, for your unwavering dedication, fervor, and steadfast commitment to enhancing earthquake resilience. May this book stand as evidence of our combined endeavors to comprehend, endure, and prosper in the presence of nature's most formidable forces.

Copyright Notice

© [2024] [Esther D. Ross]. All rights reserved.

No part of this book may be reproduced, stored in a retrieval system, or transmitted, in any form or by any means, electronic, mechanical, photocopying, recording, or otherwise, without the prior written permission of the copyright owner, except in the case of brief quotations embodied in critical reviews and certain other noncommercial uses permitted by copyright law.

CONTENT:

Introduction _____ 9

The Science Behind Earthquakes _____ 13

Historical Accounts of Devastating Earthquakes _____ 20

Plate Tectonics: The Driving Force of Earthquakes _____ 25

Assessing Earthquake Risk: Where and When They Strike _____ 30

Engineering Solutions: Building Resilient Structures _____ 37

Early Warning Systems: Saving Lives with Technology _____ 43

Coping with Trauma: Mental Health After an Earthquake _____ 48

Emergency Preparedness: Creating a Survival Plan _____ 55

Search and Rescue Operations: Heroes Amidst Rubble _____ 64

Rebuilding Communities: Restoring Hope After Disaster _____ 70

The Economic Impact of Earthquakes: Rebuilding the Economy _ 76

Environmental Consequences: Restoring Balance to Nature ____ 82

Global Collaboration: Working Together for Earthquake Resilience _____ 88

Learning from the Past: Lessons for the Future _____ 93

Beyond Earthquakes: Adapting to a Changing World _____ 98

INTRODUCTION:

Earthquakes are among the most amazing and terrifying happenings in the great theater of natural phenomena. These seismic shocks, which are a result of the Earth's erratic movements, have the immediate ability to alter entire landscapes, upend entire communities, and completely redefine lives. "Tremors of the Earth" invites you to take a trip into the center of this mysterious power, revealing the human spirit's ability to bounce back from calamities while also helping to solve the riddles of earthquakes.

Tectonic plates, which are constantly moving and colliding, float on a sea of molten rock at the center of our globe, creating a dynamic and constantly evolving environment. With their slow but unstoppable dance, these unseen and unfelt geological giants set the pace for our planet. However, when strains and tensions get too much, the Earth releases its stored anger in the form of seismic waves that rip over continents and leave destruction in their wake.

The source of earthquakes is located far below the surface of the Earth, where extreme pressures and temperatures combine to change solid rock into a liquid-like substance. Melting rock churns and convects here in the roiling depths of the mantle, propelling the movement of the tectonic plates above. Friction develops along the edges of these plates when they diverge or grind against one another, accumulating enormous amounts of energy like a coiled spring that is ready to be released.

The Earth's crust cracks along fault lines when the strain gets too high, releasing a seismic energy storm that echoes through the ground and shocks everything in its path. Buildings fall, mountainsides crumble, and the whole fabric of the Earth's surface is torn apart in an instant. It is an untainted and primordial exhibition of nature's might, one that humbles even the greatest feats of humankind.

A ray of optimism does, however, shine through the chaos and devastation, demonstrating the human spirit's ability to persevere in the face of difficulty. Following an earthquake, communities come together with the shared goal of rebuilding and healing. Unknown individuals become into neighbors by offering assistance to people in need, and volunteers and emergency responders put up endless effort to support and assist the affected.

The actual strength of humanity is most evident during these dark times, illuminating the way forward with bravery, compassion, and resiliency. We persevere through innumerable hardships, rising from the ruins stronger and more unified than before. Having been forged in the furnace of hardship, we take comfort in the ties that bind us, finding strength in our common humanity and the unwavering optimism that each of us carries within.

Tremors of the Earth extends an invitation for you to join us on this incredible adventure as we delve into the secrets of the planet's interior and examine how resilient the human spirit can be when confronted with the fury of the natural world. Come explore the mystery of earthquakes and the unbreakable energy that resides within each of us, from the blazing depths of the Earth's core to the broken remains of once-thriving communities.

Chapter 1: The Science Behind Earthquakes

Earthquakes, which are both awe-inspiring and frequently terrible occurrences, are not solely arbitrary manifestations of natural disorder. However, they represent the observable expressions of complex geological phenomena occurring at significant depths beneath the Earth's crust. This chapter delves into an exploration of the underlying principles responsible for earthquakes, encompassing the continuous motion of tectonic plates and the catastrophic release of seismic energy. Comprehending the scientific principles underlying earthquakes is not solely a subject of scholarly curiosity, but also of paramount importance in forecasting, preparing for, and alleviating the catastrophic consequences of these geological phenomena.

The fundamental basis of earthquake dynamics is rooted in the continuous interaction of Earth's tectonic plates. The Earth's lithosphere, which is its outermost layer, is fragmented into numerous tectonic plates, both vast and small in size. The movement of these plates is continuous, albeit at a gradual rate, propelled by the high-temperature convection occurring within the Earth's mantle. The interfaces where these tectonic plates converge are regions of heightened geological activity, characterized by the occurrence of seismic events, volcanic eruptions, and the formation of mountains.

A transform boundary is a prevalent type of plate boundary where earthquakes frequently occur. In this scenario, two tectonic plates undergo horizontal sliding motion. The presence of friction between the plates hinders the seamless motion, resulting in the gradual building of tension. Ultimately, the tension surpasses the rock's strength, leading to a sudden rupture and subsequently triggering an earthquake.

A convergent boundary is another form of plate boundary where earthquakes occur, characterized by the movement of two plates towards each other. The phenomenon of subduction occurs when an oceanic plate undergoes collision with a continental plate, resulting in the displacement of the denser oceanic plate beneath the continental plate. Subduction generates significant pressure and heat, which can result in the buildup of tension and the subsequent release of energy in the form of earthquakes, occasionally accompanied by volcanic activity.

In contrast, earthquakes are frequently observed along divergent borders, where two tectonic plates separate from each other. As the tectonic plates divide, magma originating from the mantle ascends to occupy the void, thereby generating fresh crust. Seismic activity can be generated along these borders due to the movement of magma and the subsequent adjustment of the surrounding rocks.

Earthquakes release seismic energy when the stress generated along a fault surpasses the strength of the rocks, resulting in their fracture and slippage. The location on the Earth's surface just above the rupture, known as the epicenter, is referred to as the focus or hypocenter. The seismic energy emitted by an earthquake propagates in the form of seismic waves, resulting in ground shaking and subsequent devastation inside the impacted region.

Seismic waves manifest in various forms, each possessing distinct features and corresponding impacts. P-waves, also known as primary waves, are the most rapid seismic waves and propagate through many substances such as solids, liquids, and gases. These waves induce compression and expansion of the ground in the direction of their motion. Secondary waves, also known as S-waves, propagate at reduced velocities subsequent to P-waves, exclusively traversing solid substances. The propagation of these waves induces a perpendicular displacement of the ground, resulting in the vibration of structures and infrastructure. Surface waves, characterized by their propagation along the Earth's surface, have a slower velocity compared to both P-waves and S-waves. However, their bigger amplitudes render them capable of inflicting substantial harm.

The determination of an earthquake's magnitude, which quantifies its size and energy release, is accomplished by the utilization of seismographs, which are sensors designed to capture ground motion. The Richter scale, devised by Charles F. Richter in 1935, is a widely employed tool for quantifying the magnitude of earthquakes. The scale used in this context is logarithmic, indicating that for every whole number increment, there is a corresponding tenfold rise in the amplitude of seismic waves and an approximate release of 31.6 times more energy. Nevertheless, contemporary seismologists frequently employ the moment magnitude scale (Mw) as a means to obtain a more precise assessment of the overall energy dissipated during an earthquake.

Scientists face a huge challenge in accurately predicting earthquakes due to the intricate geological mechanisms that drive seismic activity, which are not yet completely comprehended. Nevertheless, technological advancements and the establishment of advanced monitoring networks have enhanced our capacity to predict the probability of earthquakes in specific areas and issue timely alerts to mitigate their consequences. Methods such as the quantification of ground deformation, the surveillance of fluctuations in groundwater levels, and the examination of foreshocks might yield significant information regarding the probability of an imminent seismic event.

To effectively reduce the effects of earthquakes, a comprehensive strategy is needed that involves various fields such as engineering, urban planning, public policy, and community preparedness. Construction regulations and standards that are specifically intended to resist seismic forces have the potential to mitigate structural damage and minimize casualties in the event of an earthquake. The mitigation of seismic hazards in sensitive populations can be achieved by the implementation of land-use planning and zoning restrictions. Individuals and communities can be empowered to take proactive measures to prepare for earthquakes through public education and awareness campaigns. These measures may include securing furniture, creating emergency kits, and developing evacuation plans.

In conclusion, earthquakes are not arbitrary occurrences but rather the outcome of intricate geological phenomena propelled by the continuous motion of Earth's tectonic plates. Comprehending the scientific principles underlying earthquakes is crucial in order to forecast, plan for, and alleviate the catastrophic consequences of these geological phenomena. Although it is impossible to completely eradicate the risk of earthquakes, continuous research and preparedness initiatives can assist us in constructing more robust communities and mitigating the loss of life and property in areas prone to earthquakes.

Chapter 2: Historical Accounts of Devastating Earthquakes

Across the chronicles of time, mankind has confronted the remarkable yet alarming force of earthquakes. These seismic occurrences, frequently abrupt and uncertain, have made lasting impressions on civilizations, influencing the trajectory of human history via devastation, calamity, and fortitude. From the historical records of ancient Greece to the contemporary day, earthquakes have functioned as indicators of both calamity and fortitude, shedding light on the vulnerability of human existence when confronted with natural phenomena that are beyond our influence.

An earthquake that occurred at Sparta, Greece in 464 BC is one of the oldest recorded in history. This seismic event was documented by the esteemed ancient historian Thucydides. The tremors disrupted the peacefulness of Spartan existence, causing the collapse of structures and the loss of lives, resulting in a landscape of destruction. Within the historical records of ancient Greece, this seismic event serves as a witness to the unpredictable characteristics of the Earth and the susceptibility of human society to its destructive forces.

In the year 1755, the city of Lisbon, Portugal, saw a seismic event that stands as one of the most devastating earthquakes documented in human history. The seismic event occurred on the morning of All Saints' Day, with an estimated magnitude ranging from 8.5 to 9.0, resulting in significant devastation inside the urban area. The buildings disintegrated, the streets burst, and uncontrolled fires engulfed entire districts. As the city struggled to comprehend the enormity of the catastrophe, a colossal tsunami surged towards the land, exacerbating the disorder and devastation. The destruction of Lisbon sparked profound investigations into the essence of suffering and the presence of a compassionate deity, which posed a challenge to the dominant religious and philosophical convictions of that day.

In a more localized context, the 1906 San Francisco earthquake continues to be deeply ingrained in the collective consciousness of the American populace, serving as a poignant testament to the capricious power of natural phenomena. The earthquake, measuring 7.9 on the Richter scale, caused significant seismic activity along the well-known San Andreas Fault, resulting in extensive devastation throughout the urban area. San Francisco's renowned skyline was turned to ruins as skyscrapers disintegrated and fires engulfed entire blocks. Following the catastrophe, the city's residents demonstrated remarkable fortitude as they undertook a significant endeavor to reconstruct and recuperate. The process of reconstruction stimulated advancements in the fields of earthquake engineering and urban planning, establishing the foundation for subsequent generations to effectively address the hazards associated with seismic events.

The 2010 earthquake in Haiti serves as a significant reminder of the unequal consequences of seismic occurrences on groups that are particularly susceptible. With a magnitude of 7.0, the earthquake caused extensive damage to the impoverished nation, resulting in widespread destruction. Residences were reduced to ruins, educational institutions disintegrated, and critical infrastructure became inaccessible. The human casualty was immense, with hundreds of thousands deceased or wounded and countless others forced to leave their homes. The aftermath of the crisis, encompassing both internal and international perspectives, has exposed the underlying systemic challenges of poverty, corruption, and inequality that persistently afflict Haiti in the present era.

The historical records highlight the persistent danger presented by earthquakes and emphasize the necessity of being prepared and resilient when confronted with natural calamities. The historical lessons provide valuable guidance for future endeavors, emphasizing the significance of comprehending the intricacies of seismic risk and striving towards the construction of communities that are both safer and more robust. By means of innovation, education, and collaboration, it is possible to strive towards reducing the consequences of earthquakes and establishing a more stable and environmentally friendly future for society as a whole.

Chapter 3: Plate Tectonics: The Driving Force of Earthquakes

The captivating ballet of tectonic plates, which orchestrates seismic motions that sculpt the surface of the globe, is at the center of the geological dynamics that occur on Earth. In this chapter, we delve into the complicated ballet that is the lithosphere of the Earth, as well as the significant repercussions of the interactions that occur between these enormous plates, which eventually result in earthquakes.

The lithosphere of the Earth is similar to a massive jigsaw puzzle in that it is made up of a multitude of large and small tectonic plates that are floating on top of the semi-fluid asthenosphere that lies beneath it. These plates are constantly moving because they are propelled by the convection currents and thermal energies that are emanating from the interior of the Earth. These energies are the result of processes such as radioactive decay and residual heat from the Earth's primordial formation.

The points at which these tectonic plates meet are the epicenters of geological upheaval. It is at these points that earthquakes, volcanic eruptions, and the formation of mountain ranges take place. There are three basic manifestations of these plate borders: divergent boundaries, which occur when plates separate from one another; convergent boundaries, which occur when plates impact with one another; and transform boundaries, which occur when plates grind past each other laterally.

The renowned Mid-Atlantic Ridge is a prime example of divergent boundaries, which demonstrate the upwelling of liquid lava from the mantle, resulting in the formation of new crust as the plates move apart. Despite the fact that earthquakes that occur at divergent borders often register as modest shakes, the closeness of these earthquakes to volcanic activity offers real threats to the communities that are adjacent to them.

The crucible of seismic ferocity, which is known as convergent boundaries, is a testament to the catastrophic collision and compression of the Earth's crust. Subduction zones, which are regions in which an oceanic plate slips beneath a continental plate, are considered to be precursors to mega-thrust earthquakes, which are defined as earthquakes with magnitudes that are more than 9.0 on the Richter scale. The terrible story of the earthquake and tsunami that occurred in the Indian Ocean in 2004, which occurred in a subduction zone close to Sumatra, Indonesia, is a powerful illustration of the devastation that can be caused by powerful occurrences of this magnitude.

Typical examples of transform boundaries include the San Andreas Fault in California, which is a prime example of lateral plate motion. This type of boundary encourages the accumulation of stress, which in turn leads to the release of seismic energy. Although transform boundaries may not produce the most massive earthquakes, they have the ability to cause enormous damage, as seen by the devastating earthquake that occurred in San Francisco in 1906.

By gaining an understanding of the dynamic dance of plate tectonics and the peculiarities of unique plate boundaries, scientists are able to accurately assess the seismic risk, which in turn facilitates the development of measures for earthquake preparedness and mitigation. The purpose of this endeavor is to strengthen our collective resilience and reduce the damage that earthquakes have on communities that are vulnerable to them. This will be accomplished via persistent investigation and diligent monitoring.

Plate tectonics is the maestro who conducts the symphony of seismicity, and it reigns supreme in the theater of the geological story that is the Earth. As the human race works to traverse the tremors and tumults of our dynamic planet, the exposition of these core principles provides us with the knowledge and foresight that is necessary for constructing a safer and more resilient tomorrow in the midst of the ever-changing tectonic tableau.

Chapter 4: Assessing Earthquake Risk: Where and When They Strike

Having a comprehensive understanding of the complex geography of earthquake risk is absolutely necessary for developing effective strategies for disaster preparedness and mitigation. Within this chapter, we look into the myriad of components that contribute to seismic hazard and investigate the approaches that are utilized to analyze the chance of earthquakes occurring across a variety of places as well as the possible impact that they could have.

The tectonic setting of a particular region is a significant factor that plays a role in determining the likelihood of earthquakes occurring there. Inherently, regions that are close to the boundary of tectonic plates, such as the Pacific Ring of Fire, are prone to experiencing increased seismic activity as a result of the interaction of numerous plates. An heightened seismic hazard can be identified by a number of characteristics, including transform faults, subduction zones, and zones of continental collision.

On the other hand, earthquakes can also occur in areas that are located far away from plate boundaries and are referred to as intraplate areas. These seismic occurrences frequently originate from geologically weak zones or faults that have been present for a very long time beneath the crust of the Earth. Examples of such zones are the New Madrid seismic zone and the central United States. Although they occur less frequently than earthquakes that occur near plate boundaries, seismic events that occur within plates nonetheless pose significant dangers to the populations and infrastructure that are located nearby.

When it comes to estimating earthquake vulnerability, the built environment plays a significant influence, in addition to the geological factors that are taken into consideration. Particularly vulnerable to the detrimental impacts of seismic shaking are urban centers that are characterized by dense populations and building codes that are inadequate. Ground motion is made worse by soils that are soft and unconsolidated, and buildings and infrastructure that are not constructed properly are more likely to collapse or experience serious damage.

The development of approaches for assessing seismic hazards has provided scientists with the ability to more accurately forecast the likelihood of earthquakes occurring in a variety of locations and the severity of their effects. Probabilistic seismic hazard models combine geological, geophysical, and historical facts in order to forecast the chance of ground shaking exceeding particular thresholds during a given timeframe. A timescale is specified. These models provide politicians, engineers, and emergency planners with insights that allow them to identify high-risk areas and prioritize efforts to mitigate those risks.

In recent years, the introduction of early warning technologies has resulted in an increase in the protective envelope that is available to populations who are vulnerable. These systems are able to detect the earliest waves of an earthquake by utilizing real-time data obtained from seismic networks. They provide a warning that is anywhere from seconds to minutes in advance, before the tremors spread to places with a high population density. Early warning systems have the ability to reduce fatality rates and lessen the impact that earthquakes have on essential infrastructure and facilities, despite the fact that they are not universally prevalent.

Through the integration of geological expertise with cutting-edge technology, we are able to enhance our understanding of the dangers that earthquakes present and find ways to limit their effects. Within regions that are prone to earthquakes, we have the ability to encourage the development of communities that are safer and more sustainable through the implementation of proactive planning, the transmission of public awareness, and the investment in reliable infrastructure.

Efforts to improve earthquake resilience go beyond scientific research and technical innovation; they also include the development of robust policy frameworks and activities to engage the community. For the purpose of cultivating a culture of preparedness and resilience, it is vital for governmental agencies, academic institutions, non-governmental groups, and local communities to work together on projects.

In order to enable individuals and communities to understand the hazards that are posed by earthquakes and to take preventative actions to lessen those risks, public education initiatives play a crucial role. Many different kinds of activities can be included in awareness-raising projects. Some examples of these activities are instructional workshops, simulation exercises, and the distribution of educational materials that are adapted to a variety of different audiences.

In addition, the promotion of collaboration across disciplines is of the utmost importance in regard to the advancement of our understanding of earthquake risk and the development of effective measures for mitigation. Geologists, seismologists, engineers, urban planners, and policymakers all need to collaborate in order to incorporate a wide range of perspectives and areas of expertise into complete risk assessment and management frameworks.

An additional essential component of earthquake preparedness and mitigation measures is the investment in infrastructure that is resilient with earthquakes. There is a large reduction in the possibility for loss of life and property damage during earthquakes that can be achieved by retrofitting existing buildings to withstand seismic forces, enacting severe building rules for new construction, and strengthening essential infrastructure such as bridges, hospitals, and power plants.

When it comes to tackling transboundary seismic risks and improving catastrophe resilience on a global scale, international cooperation is also an extremely important factor. It is possible to facilitate the creation of more robust early warning systems, improve seismic hazard assessment procedures, and strengthen disaster response capabilities in sensitive locations by sharing data, best practices, and technical experience across international borders.

In conclusion, determining the likelihood of an earthquake involves a multidimensional strategy that takes into account geological knowledge, technological advancement, policy action, community involvement, and international collaboration. We can improve our ability to predict earthquakes, prepare for them, and reduce their effects by harnessing the combined skills and resources of a wide variety of stakeholders. This will ultimately result in the construction of societies that are safer and more robust for future generations.

Chapter 5: Engineering Solutions: Building Resilient Structures

The possibility of earthquakes is always present in areas that are prone to seismic activity. These earthquakes pose a considerable risk to the structural integrity and safety of buildings, bridges, and other forms of infrastructure. Nevertheless, we are able to strengthen our constructions against the overwhelming forces of nature by employing the inventiveness of engineering. This chapter delves into the complex world of earthquake-resistant design, illuminating the fundamental ideas and cutting-edge techniques that enable the building of robust structures that are able to endure the onslaught of seismic activity.

In order to design buildings that are resistant to earthquakes, it is essential to have a comprehensive understanding of the dynamic forces that are released by seismic waves upon structures. These forces, which present themselves as lateral displacement, vertical acceleration, and torsional rotation, have the capacity to deform and even disintegrate structures that are not appropriately reinforced. Engineers make use of a wide variety of tactics in order to combat these dangers, thereby assuring the well-being of the people who live there and making sure that essential assets are protected.

The concept of ductility, which exemplifies a structure's capacity to undergo significant deformations without succumbing to catastrophic failure, is essential to the design of earthquake-resistant structures. Steel and reinforced concrete are two examples of materials that are able to withstand the effects of seismic activity and serve as sturdy protectors against seismic disasters. They have the ability to bend and yield without breaking under the pressure of the strain, which is made possible by their pliability, which gives structures the resilience to withstand powerful seismic forces.

Seismic bracing and damping systems are crucial partners in the process of fortifying structures against seismic perturbations. These systems enhance the structural integrity of buildings. Seismic bracing elements, which include shear walls and cross-bracing, perform the function of steadfast sentinels by dispersing lateral stresses and providing protection against structural compromise. Damping systems, which can range from tuned mass dampers to viscous dampers, are a useful complement to these. These damping systems make use of the power of energy dissipation to dampen vibrations and prevent the possibility of resonance.

When it comes to designing buildings that are resistant to earthquakes, site-specific considerations are of the utmost importance, especially when combined with structural fortifications. During the process of designing foundations and support systems, engineers are required to take into careful consideration the local soil conditions, topography, and seismicity. By employing seismic isolation techniques, such as base isolation and flexible foundations, it is possible to facilitate the separation of structures from ground motion. This, in turn, reduces the propagation of seismic forces and strengthens the resilience of the structure against earthquakes.

As a result of the development of sophisticated modeling and simulation tools, earthquake engineering has undergone a seismic shift. These technologies have provided engineers with insights into the behavior of structures under a variety of seismic conditions that have never been offered before. The use of computer-aided design (CAD) software and finite element analysis (FEA) gives engineers the ability to maximize the performance of structures while simultaneously reducing the amount of money spent on construction and the impact they have on the environment. The cutting-edge tools that engineers have at their disposal allow them to conceive of, develop, and bring into existence structures that are able to withstand the destructive effects of seismic activity.

Engineers play a vital role in limiting the dangers posed by earthquakes and creating resilience in communities that are located in seismic hotspots. They do this by incorporating these ideas and practices into the fabric of building and infrastructure design. We go on a journey toward a future that is safer and more sustainable for everyone all around the world by working together on projects and being relentless in our pursuit of innovation.

In conclusion, the quest of design that is resistant to earthquakes is a demonstration of human creativity and a deliberate effort to bring the tumultuous forces of nature under control. Engineers are the guardians of resilience, creating structures that are able to withstand the wrath of earthquakes and protect the sanctity of human life. They are armed with a profound grasp of seismic dynamics and bolstered by creative approaches. In the process of charting a road toward a future that is filled with uncertainties, let us plow ahead with unshakable determination, crafting a landscape in which resilience reigns supreme and communities emerge stronger in the face of adversity.

Chapter 6: Early Warning Systems: Saving Lives with Technology

Technology has emerged as a formidable ally in the ongoing competition to lessen the catastrophic effects of earthquakes. Equipped with the ability to save lives and reduce damage, technology has emerged as a formidable friend. Early warning systems stand out as a very important tool among the many technical improvements that have been made. These systems provide communities with a valuable window of time to get ready for seismic occurrences and respond to them before they cause widespread destruction. This chapter examines the development, deployment, and efficiency of early warning systems in earthquake-prone locations around the world. It also highlights the crucial role that these systems play in disaster preparedness and response.

The essential idea that underpins the operation of early warning systems is the detection of the initial seismic waves that are produced by an earthquake and the prompt dissemination of warnings to populations that are most at danger. For the purpose of detecting ground motion and estimating critical factors such as the location, size, and expected intensity of an earthquake, these systems rely on complex networks of seismometers and accelerometers that are strategically put in seismically active locations.

The speed with which seismic waves travel makes it possible to identify earthquakes in a timely manner, prior to the arrival of secondary waves that are more destructive. By examining the features of the initial P-waves, early warning systems are able to swiftly determine the size and position of the earthquake. This provides essential seconds to minutes of notice to locations that are likely to experience strong shaking.

With the launch of its first nationwide system in 2007, Japan has established itself as a pioneer in the field of early warning system development and implementation. Since then, the Earthquake Early Warning (EEW) system that is operated by the Japan Meteorological Agency has become an essential component of earthquake preparedness in the nation. This system sends out notifications to millions of citizens through a variety of communication channels, such as television, radio, and mobile phones.

Early warning systems have also been implemented in a number of other nations, including the United States of America, Taiwan, and Mexico, with varied degrees of effectiveness. The Sistema de Alerta Sísmica Mexicano (SASMEX) in Mexico has received praise for its significant contribution in preventing fatalities after a number of earthquakes, including the deadly earthquake that occurred in Puebla in 2017. In a similar manner, the Earthquake Early Warning (EEW) system is managed by Taiwan's Central Weather Bureau. This system provides notifications through a variety of media outlets and mobile applications.

In the United States, the ShakeAlert system, which is operated by the United States Geological Survey (USGS), is functioning with the intention of providing early warning of earthquakes for the states of California, Oregon, and Washington, which are located on the West Coast. ShakeAlert has already demonstrated its capacity to provide important seconds to minutes of notice prior to the occurrence of shaking. This enables actions such as the automatic shutdown of key infrastructure and the notification of emergency responders. ShakeAlert is still in the process of being fully implemented.

Despite the fact that they are effective, early warning systems face a number of obstacles, such as those pertaining to funding, technical limits, and public awareness. System operators and policymakers alike continue to place a high importance on ensuring the dependability and accuracy of alerts, as well as addressing groups that are particularly vulnerable.

As technological advancements continue, early warning systems have the potential to become important instruments for mitigating the effects of earthquakes and protecting people's lives. Through the allocation of resources to research, infrastructure, and public education, we have the ability to strengthen these systems and create populations that are more resilient in areas that are prone to earthquakes.

In conclusion, early warning systems function as a ray of hope in the midst of the unpredictability that is associated with seismic events. In the context of attempts to reduce the risk of natural disasters all over the world, their ability to deliver timely alerts and enable preventative steps highlights the value of these systems. We have the ability to harness the full potential of technology to improve early warning systems and strengthen our collective resilience in the face of earthquakes and other natural disasters if we maintain our commitment to research and development and continue to innovate constantly.

Chapter 7: Coping with Trauma: Mental Health After an Earthquake

Beyond the rubble and debris that litter the terrain, the aftermath of an earthquake reaches well beyond the boundaries of the landscape. Behind the obvious devastation is a significant and mostly unsaid toll that has been taken on individual mental health. Within this chapter, we look into the psychological impact that earthquakes have on individuals as well as communities, and we investigate several ways for coping with and rebuilding after such seismic disasters.

It is possible for living through an earthquake to be a profoundly traumatic event, leaving survivors to struggle with feelings of fear, anxiety, and powerlessness. A person's sense of safety and security can be shattered when they experience tragedies such as the collapse of buildings, the death of loved ones, and the disruption of their familiar surroundings. Aftershocks continue to be a possibility even after the ground has stopped shaking, which can prolong emotions of anxiety and uncertainty for a considerable amount of time after the primary event has gone.

One of the most prevalent psychological reactions that people have in response to earthquakes and other natural catastrophes is the development of post-traumatic stress disorder (PTSD). Intrusive thoughts, flashbacks, and emotional numbing are some of the ways on which it shows itself. Survivors may also struggle with symptoms of depression, anxiety, and sleep difficulties, which can further exacerbate their anguish and make it more difficult for them to function in day-to-day life. When it comes to the psychological repercussions of earthquakes, children, in particular, bear a huge burden that is disproportionately high. It is possible that they may have difficulty comprehending and processing the developing events, that their routines will be interrupted, that they will be separated from their caregivers, and that they will be exposed to horrific pictures or stories that reinforce their vulnerability and undermine their sense of trust and safety.

Furthermore, earthquakes have the potential to have long-term effects on both the mental health and well-being of individuals. Communities that have been impacted by the disaster may experience feelings of loneliness, hopelessness, and despair as a result of being displaced, losing their livelihoods, and experiencing social disturbance. The weakening of communities and the deterioration of their cultural legacy further undermines the resilience and cohesiveness of societies that are already struggling to recover from the aftermath of a disaster.

In the aftermath of an earthquake, there are opportunities for resiliency and healing, despite the enormous challenges that have been presented. Psychosocial support services, which include counseling, support groups, and community outreach programs, provide survivors with a secure environment in which they can express their feelings, have the opportunity to talk about their experiences, and receive validation and support from their peers who have been through similar challenges.

In order to effectively meet the varied requirements of the communities that have been impacted, it is necessary to implement interventions that are culturally sensitive and that combine indigenous knowledge and traditional healing practitioners. These treatments empower survivors and encourage the development of social connections and support networks by recognizing cultural beliefs and values and engaging local stakeholders in the recovery process. In addition, they honor the cultural beliefs and values of the community.

The recovery process following an earthquake requires more than just the rehabilitation of physical structures; it also requires the restoration of lives and the revival of expectations. By giving mental health and well-being a higher priority in disaster planning and response activities, we may provide communities the ability to not only survive but also thrive in the face of adversity.

The provision of psychological first aid is very important in the early aftermath of an earthquake. Responders who have received training provide survivors with emotional support, comfort, and practical aid. This lays the framework for more thorough psychosocial support in the days and weeks to come. Individuals who are experiencing a crisis are helped to stabilize through this early intervention, and they are connected with additional services for sustained treatment.

As the long road to recovery begins for communities, it is essential to cultivate a feeling of collective resilience and solidarity among the people in those places. Survivors are able to draw strength from one another's experiences, share their stories, and express their feelings through the medium of support groups, which give a place for communication. Surviving individuals can find solace and affirmation in peer support networks, which serve as a reminder that they are not the only ones going through the challenges they are facing.

By incorporating cultural and spiritual traditions into psychological support therapies, it is possible to increase the effectiveness of these interventions and their relevance in a variety of cultures. Traditional ways of healing, such as telling stories, participating in ritual rites, and social gatherings, have the potential to offer solace and meaning in the midst of the chaos and uncertainty that comes with life after a calamity. Interventions that express respect for the distinctive identities and experiences of survivors by recognizing cultural traditions and values help to build a sense of belonging and connection during the recovery process.

Community-based approaches to psychosocial assistance give local inhabitants the ability to take responsibility for their own healing path and to mobilize resources within their own networks. The provision of peer counseling, the organization of support groups, and the coordination of outreach efforts are all activities that are carried out by community volunteers who have received professional training. These grassroots efforts encourage healing and repair from within by utilizing the collective wisdom and resiliency of communities. They also facilitate the strengthening of social links and the development of a feeling of optimism for the future.

In the aftermath of an earthquake, mental health and psychosocial support must be incorporated into all stages of the disaster management cycle, beginning with preparation and response and continuing through recovery and reconstruction. We are able to construct societies that are more resilient and capable of surviving the storms of misfortune and emerging stronger on the other side if we give priority to the psychological well-being of afflicted individuals and communities.

Chapter 8: Emergency Preparedness: Creating a Survival Plan

When confronted with natural disasters such as earthquakes, being well-prepared might actually mean the difference between life and death. This chapter explores the crucial relevance of disaster preparedness and provides practical guidelines for individuals, families, and communities to implement in order to develop comprehensive survival strategies that are suited to their particular requirements and circumstances.

When it comes to being prepared for an emergency, the first step is to have a thorough understanding of the dangers and weaknesses that are specific to your locality. The foundation for identifying possible hazards and prioritizing mitigation activities is laid by conducting an assessment of the risk of earthquakes occurring in your region, as well as the potential implications on infrastructure, utilities, and transportation networks.

After gaining an understanding of these dangers, the next stage is to devise a complete survival strategy. In the event of a catastrophe, this plan must to include supplies for shelter, food, water, medical treatment, and communication, in addition to techniques for evacuating and reuniting individuals who have been separated.

Any survival plan should begin with the accumulation of basic supplies as a foundational component. It is possible for people and families to survive in the aftermath of an earthquake by consuming non-perishable food products such as canned goods, dried fruits, and granola bars. This is because access to fresh food may be limited. Additionally, during extended periods of emergency, it is possible to protect one's health and well-being by ensuring that there is a sufficient supply of clean water, drugs, and first aid supplies.

The establishment of communication lines with family members, neighbors, and emergency responders is of the utmost importance, in addition to the implementation of physical supplies. During times of crisis, it is possible to hasten the process of reunification and coordination by designating a meeting spot and developing a mechanism for checking in with loved ones. Being familiar with local emergency services, such as evacuation routes and shelters, enables individuals to make decisions based on accurate information and makes it easier to obtain aid when it is required.

In order to guarantee that survival plans are effective, practice and repetition are of the utmost importance. Simulations and drills should be performed on a regular basis in order to reinforce emergency protocols and identify areas that could want improvement. Participation in these exercises by members of the family, neighbors, and organizations associated with the community encourages collaboration and teamwork, both of which are essential components during times of crisis.

The ability of a community to withstand the effects of a disaster is contingent upon the concerted efforts of individuals and organizations working together to improve disaster preparedness and response. Engaging with local emergency management agencies, volunteer groups, and neighborhood associations can result in the acquisition of vital resources and support for preparedness activities. Additionally, participation in community-wide activities such as emergency response training and neighborhood watch programs strengthens solidarity and mutual aid, both of which are essential for surviving storms.

Individuals can strengthen their resilience and increase their chances of surviving and recovering from crises by taking preventative efforts to prepare for natural catastrophes such as earthquakes and other types of natural disasters. It is of the utmost importance to keep in mind that the correct time to get ready is before a calamity occurs. Get started right away by developing a survival strategy and putting together a kit that has the necessary materials. There is no question that your future self will express gratitude to you for your foresight and preparation.

During times of crisis, emergency preparedness is not only a conceptual idea; rather, it is a practically applicable activity that has the potential to significantly influence the outcomes. It is the first step toward developing an effective survival plan for your community to have an understanding of the specific dangers and vulnerabilities that are confronting your group. It is possible for individuals to identify major hazards and prioritize mitigation actions in accordance with those hazards by evaluating the likelihood of earthquakes and the potential implications that earthquakes could have on infrastructure, utilities, and transportation networks.

After these dangers have been recognized, the following stage is to design a detailed survival plan that is adapted to your particular requirements and the conditions that you are currently facing. In the event of a catastrophe, this plan must to include supplies for shelter, food, water, medical treatment, and communication, in addition to techniques for evacuating and reuniting individuals who have been separated.

Making sure you have enough of the things you need to survive is a vital part of any survival plan. It is possible to offer sustenance in the days following an earthquake by utilizing non-perishable food items such as canned foods, dried fruits, and granola bars. This is because access to fresh food may be limited at this time. In the same vein, keeping a sufficient quantity of clean water, medications, and first aid supplies on hand can be of great assistance in ensuring one's health and safety during an extended emergency situation.

The establishment of communication lines with family members, neighbors, and emergency responders is crucial, in addition to the provision of physical supplies. During times of crisis, it can be helpful to designate a meeting site and establish a method for checking in with loved ones. This can make it easier to reunite with loved ones and coordinate their actions. In addition, becoming familiar with local emergency services, such as evacuation routes and emergency shelters, can assist in making well-informed decisions and gaining access to support when it is required.

When it comes to ensuring that your survival plan is effective, both practice and repetition are essential components. Regularly practicing and simulating emergency procedures can be an effective way to reinforce existing protocols and pinpoint areas that could use improvement. When dealing with a crisis, it is important to consider the possibility of incorporating family members, neighbors, and community organizations in these exercises. This will help to build collaboration and teamwork.

The ability of a community to withstand the effects of a disaster is contingent upon the concerted efforts of individuals and organizations working together to both prepare for and respond to such events. When it comes to your attempts to be prepared, collaborating with local emergency management organizations, volunteer groups, and neighborhood associations can provide you with vital tools and support. Participating in community-wide activities, such as emergency response training and neighborhood watch programs, can also assist establish the links of solidarity and mutual aid that are necessary for weathering the storm. These are vital for surviving the storm.

Enhancing your resilience and improving your chances of surviving and recovering from a crisis can be accomplished by taking preventative measures to get ready for natural disasters such as earthquakes and other types of environmental catastrophes. Always keep in mind that the best time to get ready is before a calamity occurs. Begin right away by developing a survival strategy and putting together a kit that has the necessary resources. Your long-term self will be grateful to you.

Chapter 9: Search and Rescue Operations: Heroes Amidst Rubble

The unsung heroes of search and rescue operations emerge in the midst of the turmoil and damage that follows an earthquake or other natural disaster. The frontline is comprised of these courageous individuals, who are working relentlessly to rescue lives and instill hope in the hearts of those who are stuck within the destroyed structures. The complexities of their obstacles, solutions, and the unyielding tenacity that defines their goal are explored in great depth in Chapter 9.

As soon as the tremors of an earthquake are felt, search and rescue activities, often known as SAR, begin. With the urgency of the situation driving them, teams quickly organize in order to seek and rescue people who are buried beneath collapsed structures, debris, and rubble. When it comes to these efforts to save lives, time is the most formidable foe, since the likelihood of discovering survivors decreases with each passing hour.

SAR teams traverse across dangerous and inaccessible terrains in order to reach persons who are in need of assistance. They do this by employing a wide variety of procedures and gear. Urban search and rescue (USAR) units take advantage of specialized technology such as search cameras and listening devices, as well as canine units that have been educated to the point where they are able to detect any signs of life that may be hiding among the abandoned buildings. Furthermore, in order to accomplish the difficult process of clearing debris and establishing channels for rescue workers, heavy machinery such as cranes, excavators, and hydraulic cutters prove to be vital.

It is essential for search and rescue efforts to be coordinated and communicated with one another in a fluid manner across the numerous agencies and players involved. Incident Command Systems (ICS) are the key, providing a formal framework for organizing and managing the complex network of rescue activities. They serve as the linchpin. Within the confines of this structure, distinct lines of authority and accountability are formed, which guarantees a cohesive approach within the context of the shared objective of saving lives. It is possible to maximize the usage of resources and knowledge through the employment of interagency coordination, which is supported by mutual aid agreements and partnerships with international relief groups. This collaboration increases the efficiency of search and rescue operations.

The determination of search and rescue teams is completely unwavering, even in the face of the severe challenges they face. They toil relentlessly, frequently around the clock, and do so in dangerous settings in order to bring hope to others who are in a state of despair. In communities that have been destroyed by calamity, their bravery and altruism serve as a source of inspiration, sparking a sense of perseverance and fortitude among the people. They are a living example of the immense influence that compassion and unity can have in the face of hardship, as demonstrated by their unrelenting determination.

In addition to their efforts to save lives, search and rescue teams also serve as essential sources of intelligence by carefully evaluating the impact of the disaster and the number of casualties that have occurred in the impacted areas. The response and recovery operations that are being choreographed by government agencies, humanitarian groups, and emergency responders are built on the foundation of this vital information, which acts as the backbone. One of the most important roles that search and rescue teams play in accelerating the process of rebuilding broken lives and communities is diverting resources to the areas where they are most needed.

When it comes to search and rescue operations, preparation and training are the cornerstones that provide lightning-fast and efficient responses to earthquakes and other types of disasters. Essential abilities, like as search procedures, medical triage, and technical rescue operations, can be honed through the use of regular drills, simulations, and exercises. Furthermore, search and rescue teams are able to maintain their position at the forefront of innovation by continuously refining their techniques and embracing best practices in disaster response. This is made possible by engagement in ongoing professional development and collaboration with foreign counterparts.

The tenacious spirit of search and rescue teams shines brilliantly in times of disaster, exemplifying the essence of compassion, courage, and resilience in its purest form. As they embark on the tough journey of reconstructing lives amidst the ruins, their steadfast determination and sacrifices serve as a monument to the strength of human solidarity, transcending boundaries and unifying communities in the process. As the dust begins to settle and hope begins to emerge, it is the relentless efforts of these unsung heroes that shed light on the route that leads to rehabilitation and rejuvenation.

Chapter 10: Rebuilding Communities: Restoring Hope After Disaster

The environment is ravaged by destruction in the aftermath of a seismic upheaval, and the human spirit is put to the test in ways that are beyond anybody's ability to picture. The purpose of this chapter is to dive into the complicated process of post-disaster recovery, which goes beyond the simple repair of physical structures and include the restoration of communities, livelihoods, and hope. It investigates the complicated dance that takes place between resiliency and renewal, elaborating on the difficulties and opportunities that are inherent in the process of reconstructing the social fabric of communities that have been devastated by earthquakes.

There is a symphony of chaos and sadness in the immediate aftermath of the event. A number of lives were shattered, homes were turned to rubble, and important services were disrupted. Nevertheless, a tenacious spirit may be found within the wreckage, a communal will to emerge from the rubble and restore what was lost. Resilience is the foundation upon which the recovery process is built, serving as a guiding light that points communities in the direction of a more promising future.

Before beginning any recovery efforts, a thorough assessment of the damage and a determination of the urgent requirements must be carried out. In order to offer survivors with emergency shelter, food, water, and medical care, government agencies, humanitarian organizations, and local community groups have come together to work together in a joint effort. A key refuge for individuals who have been displaced as a result of the calamity is the establishment of temporary shelters, which can take the form of anything from tents to prefabricated housing units and community centers.

As the first shock wears off, the focus shifts to the massive work of long-term restoration, which includes the rehabilitation of houses, schools, hospitals, and other essential infrastructure. It is necessary to engage in careful planning, coordination, and major investment during this phase in order to guarantee that the newly constructed buildings will not only be restored, but will also be equipped with the ability to withstand future seismic events. It is of the utmost importance that community engagement and consultation become linchpins in the process of developing ownership and trust in the rebuilding process. This ensures that the impacted population plays an active role in shaping their destiny.

The comprehensive approach to recovery include not only the physical rehabilitation of the affected area, but also the social, economic, and psychological repercussions that have resulted from the earthquake. By providing survivors with psychosocial support services, counseling, and trauma-informed care, it is possible to assist them in coping with the emotional toll that the disaster has had on them and in rebuilding their lives after it has been broken. Both individuals and businesses are given the ability to not only recover from the crisis but also to grow as a result of the economic recovery programs, livelihood support, and microfinance initiatives that are being implemented simultaneously.

The foundation of community resilience is comprised of the bedrock of solidarity, cooperation, and mutual support among its members. It is the grassroots initiatives that take center stage, which include everything from community-led reconstruction projects to the development of neighborhood associations and mutual help networks. The citizens are given the ability to take charge of their own healing and actively participate in the process of determining the future course of their communities through these activities. Communities have the ability to rebuild not simply as faithful reproductions of the past, but rather as entities that are more robust, more inclusive, and more sustainable if they make use of the local knowledge, resources, and social capital.

Nevertheless, the process of rebuilding is laden with difficulties everywhere you go. An insufficient amount of resources, obstacles posed by bureaucracy, and competing objectives frequently work together to obstruct progress and frustrate efforts to bring about significant change. Furthermore, the pre-existing specters of inequality, poverty, and social marginalization might worsen vulnerabilities, which in turn hinders the recovery of the groups that are the most marginalized and disadvantaged.

However, these difficulties present chances for innovation, collaboration, and transformation within the context of the situation. Using ideals of sustainable development, equity, and resilience as guiding lights is something that is advocated for in this chapter. Individual communities are strongly encouraged to emerge from disasters not simply as survivors but also as agents of constructive change. The narrative highlights that despite the challenging route that lies ahead, those who possess courage, tenacity, and solidarity have the ability to transform the desolation into a canvas against which hope can be rebuilt, so forging a future that shines brighter than it did before.

In conclusion, the process of reconstructing communities after an earthquake is a demonstration of the human capacity for resilience and the unconquerable spirit that emerges from the ashes of tragedy. This chapter sheds light on the complexity and nuances of post-disaster recovery, presenting a road map for communities to follow in order to negotiate the hurdles and seize the chances for growth, unity, and transformation. The story emphasizes that communities are capable of reestablishing optimism and forging a future that is not influenced by the shadows of calamity if they have the fortitude, perseverance, and collective commitment to solidarity to do so.

Chapter 11: The Economic Impact of Earthquakes: Rebuilding the Economy

Earthquakes, with their unpredictability, not only destroy homes and structures, but they also wreak havoc on the fragile economic fabric of nations. In the aftermath of seismic occurrences of this nature, the effects extend well beyond the original shocks, having enormous impact on people's lives, industries, and even entire nations. During the course of this chapter, we look into the myriad of economic repercussions that earthquakes have, both in the short term and in the long term, and we investigate several measures that can be utilized to repair and strengthen economies against future shocks.

Disruption and loss are the immediate consequences of this.

The landscape that is left behind after an earthquake is one that is characterized by disorder and uncertainty. Companies are compelled to cease their operations, supply networks come to a grinding halt, and the confidence of customers plummets during this time. In addition to hindering economic activity and making rescue and recovery efforts more difficult, the loss of essential infrastructure, such as roads, ports, and utilities, occurs. For the purpose of addressing urgent demands such as property damage, emergency response, and infrastructure restoration, governments are exerting a great deal of effort to mobilize resources and are stretching their budgets to their limits.

Long-Term Consequences: Effects That Are Still Present"

A lasting impression is left on the towns and regions that are impacted by earthquakes, even after the immediate turmoil has passed. At the same time that firms are on the verge of going bankrupt, displaced workers are struggling with unemployment, and investor confidence is ebbing and flowing. The destruction of human capital, cultural legacy, and social networks presents enormous obstacles to long-term recovery, which in turn impedes efforts to rebuild resilience and prosperity.

Revitalization of the economy presents opportunities in the midst of competition.

Nevertheless, somewhere in the midst of the wreckage is the possibility of economic revitalization. The efforts that are being put into reconstruction spark a demand for goods and services, which in turn creates employment opportunities and brings investment to the affected areas. In order to establish the groundwork for long-term economic development, communities should prioritize infrastructure that is both resilient and sustainable. This will help to strengthen local industries and enhance the competitiveness of the community on a global scale.

Making an Investment in Resilience: Reducing the Impact of Future Risks

When it comes to reducing the economic impact of earthquakes, prevention is of the first importance. Both the possibility of future catastrophes and the intensity of those disasters can be reduced by investments in disaster risk reduction and preparedness, which pay considerable benefits. In order to minimize losses and maximize resilience, governments and corporations can protect lives, livelihoods, and essential assets by implementing robust infrastructure, early warning systems, and community preparedness activities. This will allow them to minimize losses and maximize resilience.

In times of crisis, global solidarity may be a great source of support.

The world community's ability to work together is a ray of light that shines in the aftermath of an earthquake. Humanitarian help, technical assistance, and financial support from the international community provide an essential lifeline for regions that have been affected by a disaster. These forms of assistance bridge the gap between rapid relief and sustained regeneration. It is possible for nations to maneuver through the turbulent aftermath of earthquakes with greater resilience and determination if they create unity and teamwork among their citizens.

The Conclusion: Enhancing Resilience in Order to Achieve a Sustainable Future

When earthquakes have an effect on the economy, it serves as a sharp reminder of how interdependent we are in a society that is increasingly globalized. When it comes to protecting the economy of nations and the well-being of their populations, making investments in resilience and readiness is not just a wise choice; it is an absolute must. The strengthening of communities, businesses, and economies against the effects of seismic shocks is a step in the right direction toward a future that is more sustainable and profitable for everyone.

In a nutshell, earthquakes have a significant influence on the economy, which can be felt significantly further than the tremors themselves. Despite this, there are numerous prospects for revitalization and expansion inside the ruins. It is possible for nations to overcome the destruction caused by earthquakes and chart a road towards a more prosperous tomorrow if they make smart investments, actively collaborate with other nations, and remain unshakable in their resilience.

Chapter 12: Environmental Consequences: Restoring Balance to Nature

As a result of the enormous impact that earthquakes have on both human infrastructure and the natural environment, they bring a wide variety of opportunities and problems that are complex in nature. This chapter delves into the complex web of environmental repercussions that are caused by seismic activity. We investigate several methods that can be utilized to lessen the severity of these effects and to encourage ecological restoration in order to create a state of harmony and equilibrium in the natural world.

There is a high probability that the immediate aftermath of an earthquake will be characterized by the violent disruption of ecosystems and habitats. In addition to uprooting plants and posing a threat to biodiversity, landslides, soil liquefaction, and ground subsidence are all processes that transform landscapes. Not only does the destruction of habitats put an incalculable number of species in danger, but it also undermines the essential ecosystem services that are critical to the survival of both human societies and animal populations. Rivers and waterways that have been altering as a result of seismic pressures may flood, erode, or become clogged with sediment, which would further exacerbate the loss of habitat and compromise the quality of the water.

In addition, earthquakes have the potential to release secondary hazards such as tsunamis, landslides, and volcanic eruptions, which can increase the damage done to the environment. Coastal habitats are flooded, coral reefs are decimated, and marine life is disrupted when tsunamis are generated by earthquakes that occur beneath the ocean. As a result of landslides and volcanic eruptions, enormous swaths of land are buried by ash and debris, resulting in the destruction of forests, crops, and communities, as well as causing a chain reaction of ecological consequences.

Earthquakes, in addition to causing immediate physical destruction, have the potential to significantly impact the quality and availability of natural resources that are necessary for sustained life. It is possible for groundwater reservoirs to become contaminated with contaminants as a result of ground shaking and liquefaction, which poses long-term threats to human health and the integrity of ecosystems. The degradation of soil quality can be caused by erosion, landslides, and the deposition of ash, which can lead to a decrease in agricultural production and an increase in food insecurity. Additionally, the emission of dust, ash, and poisonous chemicals into the atmosphere can have a negative impact on the quality of the air, which can not only pose hazards to the respiratory system but also contribute to the overall degradation of the environment.

Despite this, earthquakes also give opportunities for ecological rejuvenation and restoration, even in the middle of chaotic situations. Eventually, disturbed landscapes are progressively reclaimed by successive processes, which are driven by resilient plant species and microbial communities. This process helps to support the regeneration of ecosystems over the course of time. Furthermore, creative solutions such as ecological engineering and habitat restoration have the potential to speed up this recovery process. These strategies can strengthen the natural systems' resistance to future shocks and enhance their capacity to support biodiversity and ecosystem services.

When it comes to tackling the environmental effects of earthquakes, the urgency of safeguarding and preserving biodiversity is at the center of the discussion. In addition to providing a home for a wide variety of species, healthy ecosystems also offer a number of crucial services. These services include the regulation of climate, the purification of water, and the stabilization of soils. These characteristics are essential for minimizing the effects of seismic risks and protecting human well-being. Conservation activities, such as the development of protected areas, the restoration of wildlife corridors, and the adoption of sustainable land management methods, are vital for the preservation of biodiversity hotspots and the enhancement of ecosystem resilience in regions that are prone to earthquakes.

When it comes to tackling the global dimensions of earthquake-induced environmental consequences, international cooperation and collaboration play a crucial role from a comprehensive perspective. It is possible for nations to expand their collective capacity for disaster risk reduction and environmental management through the sharing of knowledge, experience, and resources. This will result in increased resilience in places that are particularly vulnerable. In addition, it is essential to incorporate environmental factors into disaster preparedness and response planning in order to reduce the ecological damage that earthquakes do and to promote sustainable recovery and development pathways.

Recognizing the interconnectivity of natural and human systems is essential to tackling the environmental implications of earthquakes. This is the root of the problem. Through the adoption of proactive conservation measures, the promotion of ecological restoration, and the pursuit of sustainable development practices, we may work toward reestablishing a state of equilibrium in the natural world and cultivating a future that is more resilient for future generations. By doing so, we not only respect the inherent worth of biodiversity, but we also acknowledge our collective obligation to protect the Earth's priceless ecosystems for the sake of the well-being of all forms of life.

Chapter 13: Global Collaboration: Working Together for Earthquake Resilience

The unpredictability of earthquakes, which are a natural force, poses a pervasive threat that is not limited by national boundaries and necessitates concerted efforts on a worldwide scale to lessen the impact of earthquakes and strengthen resilience. In this chapter, we look into the significance of international collaboration in earthquake resilience. We throw light on a variety of projects and collaborations that are aimed at strengthening preparedness, response, and recovery measures all around the world.

It is vital that nations and regions share their expertise, data, and best practices in order to strengthen earthquake resilience. This is the core of global collaboration in earthquake resilience. The United Nations Office for Disaster Risk Reduction (UNDRR) and the International Seismological Centre (ISC) are two examples of international organizations that act as conduits for the sharing of information and collaboration regarding seismic monitoring, risk assessment, and disaster management.

The spirit of collaboration that exists among scientists and academics all around the world is exemplified by projects such as the Global Seismic Hazard Assessment Program (GSHAP) and the Global Earthquake Model (GEM). The purpose of these activities is to standardize approaches for evaluating seismic risk and to disseminate findings to different stakeholders, including policymakers, planners, and the general public. These programs improve the accuracy and reliability of earthquake risk assessments by combining resources and experience. As a result, decision-makers at the local, national, and global levels are given more influence.

The strengthening of early warning systems and disaster response skills in regions that are prone to earthquakes is equally dependent on the participation of international collaboration. The United Nations International Strategy for Disaster Reduction (UNISDR) is the driving force behind the initiatives that are being taken to encourage the creation and implementation of early warning systems in countries that are particularly vulnerable. UNISDR's provision of technical assistance and support for capacity-building helps to strengthen the effectiveness and reach of these systems, which in turn amplifies the impact that they have on saving lives.

The Pacific Tsunami Warning Center and the Caribbean Disaster Emergency Management Agency (CDEMA) are two examples of regional organizations that demonstrate the value of collaboration in the field of seismic monitoring and response coordination. The monitoring of seismic activity, the dissemination of timely notifications, and the mobilization of resources in the aftermath of earthquakes and other natural disasters are all made easier by these groups. In order to strengthen regional resilience and improve readiness and response processes, these organizations emphasize the importance of fostering cooperation among their member nations and other stakeholders.

In addition to providing technical assistance, international relationships play a pivotal role in mobilizing financial resources and providing support for efforts to strengthen earthquake disaster resilience. financing for infrastructure projects, capacity-building efforts, and grassroots programs that aim to mitigate seismic risk and strengthen resilience in vulnerable communities is provided by multilateral development banks, bilateral donors, and charitable groups. These organizations are responsible for providing financing.

The road to worldwide collaboration in earthquake resilience, on the other hand, is not devoid of obstacles. It is possible for nations and regions to be unable to coordinate and cooperate with one another due to differences in governance structures, political objectives, and the availability of resources. In addition, disparities in wealth, technology, and knowledge can exacerbate vulnerabilities and impede efforts to strengthen resilience, particularly in marginalized populations who are experiencing heightened risk.

Despite these obstacles, the necessity of international cooperation in the field of earthquake resilience continues to be unwavering. The ability of nations and regions to confront similar difficulties, share critical insights, and stimulate innovation and adaptation in the face of seismic risks can be achieved through the pooling of their collective capabilities and resources. The international community has the ability to construct a future in which the destructive impact of earthquakes is lessened and the resilience of communities all over the world is strengthened against the turbulent forces of nature via persistent partnership.

Chapter 14: Harnessing Technology: Innovations in Earthquake Resilience

Within the context of our contemporary day, technology is a tremendous ally in our ongoing fight against earthquakes and the tragic aftermath of earthquakes. This chapter digs into the cutting-edge technology and digital solutions that are redefining earthquake resilience efforts. These technologies and solutions range from early warning systems to the complexities of disaster response and recovery.

The development of early warning systems (EWS), which send out signals in real time to communities that are in danger of being affected by earthquakes, is widely considered to be one of the most significant advances in earthquake resilience. These systems are dependent on a network of sensors that are able to detect the initial seismic waves that occur during an earthquake and quickly transmit alerts through a variety of communication channels. These channels include mobile phones, radio broadcasts, and television broadcasts.

The past few years have witnessed significant advancements in sensor technology, data processing capabilities, and communication infrastructure, which have made it possible to deploy early warning systems that are becoming increasingly reliable and robust in earthquake-prone locations all over the world. Seismometers, GPS receivers, and high-precision accelerometers are the three components that are utilized by these systems in order to provide accurate measurements of ground motion. These data are analyzed in real time by sophisticated algorithms and machine learning algorithms, which allow for an accurate estimation of the size, epicenter, and potential impact of earthquakes using machine learning.

There is a significant role that mobile applications and social media platforms play in the dissemination of alerts and important emergency information to communities and individuals who are impacted by the situation. Early warning systems are able to rapidly reach a large number of people by utilizing the widespread availability of cellphones and digital connectivity. This provides those systems with valuable seconds to minutes of warning before earthquakes occur. During this priceless period of time, preventative actions can be performed, thereby reducing the impact that earthquakes have on people's lives and their means of subsistence.

In addition to early warning systems, technology is redefining efforts to respond to earthquakes and recover from seismic activity. Geographic information systems (GIS) and remote sensing technology give first responders the ability to map and assess damage, identify weaknesses in vital infrastructure, and distribute resources for relief and rescue operations. Unmanned aerial vehicles (UAVs) and drones provide aerial imagery and reconnaissance in areas that are currently inaccessible or hazardous, thereby accelerating the process of identifying survivors and assessing the extent of damage.
Additionally, digital platforms and online tools make it easier for parties involved in earthquake resilience efforts to coordinate and collaborate in a seamless manner. Volunteers

are given the ability to crowdsource real-time information regarding disaster affects, resource requirements, and response activities through the use of crisis mapping platforms such as OpenStreetMap and Ushahidi. This facilitates more effective coordination and decision-making among humanitarian organizations and responders.

Emerging technologies such as artificial intelligence (AI), the Internet of Things (IoT), and blockchain have the potential to significantly improve earthquake resilience. This is something that should be considered in the future. While Internet of Things (IoT)-enabled sensors and smart infrastructure provide real-time monitoring and feedback to strengthen the resilience of buildings, bridges, and key infrastructure, artificial intelligence (AI)-driven predictive modeling and risk assessment tools help in detecting vulnerabilities and prioritizing mitigation methods.

In the context of disaster response and recovery efforts, blockchain technology, which is distinguished by its distributed and immutable ledger system, offers potential options for boosting transparency, accountability, and trust. By facilitating transactions that are both secure and transparent, blockchain enhances the distribution of help, monitors the logistics of supply chain operations, and guarantees the timely and effective distribution of resources to those who are in the greatest need.

In the midst of seismic dangers, the technological advancements that are being displayed here have the potential to transform efforts to make buildings more earthquake-resistant and might perhaps save the lives of a great number of people. As a result of utilizing the power of digital technologies, we are able to strengthen communities, improve early warning capabilities, and refine disaster response and recovery procedures, which will ultimately reduce the damage that earthquakes have on persons, economies, and civilizat

Chapter 15: Education and Awareness: Empowering Communities for Resilience

Education and awareness are two of the most important foundations that communities may use to strengthen themselves against the devastation that earthquakes can cause. The combination of these two forces gives individuals and society the ability to recognize seismic hazards, to prepare for them, and to effectively respond to them. This chapter dives into the critical role that education and awareness play in earthquake resilience efforts, shedding light on techniques that can be utilized to disseminate information, readiness, and action throughout all levels of society.

Knowledge is essential to earthquake resilience, which can be defined as an understanding of the risks, hazards, and vulnerabilities that are specific to each environment or community. The dissemination of this information, the increasing of awareness regarding seismic dangers, and the cultivation of a culture of preparedness and resilience among individuals, families, and communities are all accomplished through education, which serves as the vanguard.

Education about earthquakes is becoming increasingly important in schools because they provide students with controlled and interactive learning environments in which they can gain knowledge about seismic science, emergency planning, and safety standards. Students become familiar with emergency protocols by participating in earthquake exercises, utilizing educational materials, and participating in outreach programs. This provides them with the information and abilities necessary to manage seismic situations in an effective manner.

Community-based education and outreach efforts take a vital role in reaching vulnerable communities and encouraging individuals to adopt proactive steps to mitigate risk and strengthen their resilience against earthquakes. These initiatives extend beyond the constraints of the classroom and expand beyond the reach of traditional educational institutions. Activities like as public awareness campaigns, workshops, and training sessions provide citizens, companies, and community groups with vital information and resources, which in turn stimulates the development and implementation of preparedness plans and measures.

The dissemination of instructional materials and information relevant to earthquake resilience can be facilitated through the use of digital platforms and online resources, which are powerful instruments that facilitate outreach to a variety of targeted populations. Increasing awareness and fostering readiness among large segments of the population can be accomplished through the use of interactive technologies, instructive videos, and informative articles that are made available through mobile applications, social media channels, and websites.

Education, which goes beyond merely increasing awareness, plays a vital part in the process of cultivating a culture of resilience. It gives individuals and communities the confidence to take collective action in order to reduce their vulnerability to earthquakes. The mobilization of resources, the cultivation of social cohesion, and the promotion of collaboration and solidarity among inhabitants are all facilitated by community-based organizations, volunteer groups, and grassroots initiatives.

For the purpose of enhancing the effectiveness of education and awareness initiatives pertaining to earthquake resilience, it is absolutely necessary to establish partnerships between governmental agencies, civil society organizations, academic institutions, and the commercial sector. To cultivate a culture of resilience that goes beyond individual preparedness to encompass collective action and societal transformation, it is possible to devise innovative and effective strategies to engage and empower communities that are at risk. These strategies can be developed by harnessing the expertise, resources, and networks of a diverse range of stakeholders.

The conclusion is that education and awareness are powerful tools that may be used to strengthen earthquake resilience and empower individuals and communities to protect themselves and their families from the dangers that are posed by seismic activity. It is possible to create a future that is more resilient by investing in education, outreach, and capacity-building activities. This future will be one that leaves the legacy of preparedness and resilience to future generations.

www.ingramcontent.com/pod-product-compliance
Lightning Source LLC
LaVergne TN
LVHW020425080526
838202LV00055B/5035